Vet

Lucy M. George

Ando Twin

Doctor Mike is a veterinarian. Just like a doctor takes care of people, Doctor Mike looks after animals, such as dogs, cats, cows, sheep, and pigs.

Today Doctor Mike is working at the vet's office.
Suddenly the phone rings!

"RRRIIIINNGG!!!"

It's Gillian, the farmer.
One of her animals
is in trouble!

There's a storm outside. The big wheels
of Doctor Mike's car splash
down the dirt road to the farm.

Gillian meets Doctor Mike
at the gate.

"This way!" she shouts over the wind,
pointing at the field. "One of my sheep
is having trouble giving birth to her lamb!"

They reach the ewe just in time. Doctor Mike kneels down in the mud to take a closer look.

"Pass my bag please, Gillian!" Doctor Mike calls. "I think the lamb is stuck!"

In the warm barn, Doctor Mike helps the ewe give birth to her lamb. The lamb is safe!

Just then, they hear a voice calling, "Mom!"

"Help, come quickly!" Gillian's daughter, Megan, calls. Doctor Mike runs to find her.

Megan's dog is trapped!

"One of Prince's legs is stuck in the chicken coop," she cries.

Prince is very upset. "Shh, boy, it's okay,"
Doctor Mike says gently.

Doctor Mike is very good with
animals, and Prince calms down.

Doctor Mike frees Prince's paw
quickly and looks at his leg.
Megan strokes Prince's head.

"Poor boy!" she says.

Prince has hurt himself, so they take him back to the clinic. He is going to need a bandage.

Doctor Mike opens his vet bag, washes his hands, and puts on his gloves.

He cleans the scrape and wraps a bandage on Prince's leg. "There you go, Prince. All better!" he says.

The next day, Doctor Mike goes back to Gillian's farm to visit the lambs.

He checks on the new lamb
and makes sure all the
others are healthy.

While he is at the farm, Doctor Mike checks the other animals too. He visits the pigs . . .

. . . and the horses.

Then Doctor Mike examines the cows. He checks their hooves, eyes, tongues, and udders. All of the animals look healthy.

Finally, Doctor Mike and Gillian go into the warm farmhouse. They are having a treat when . . .

. . . Prince bounds into the kitchen!

His leg is much better
and he's very happy to
see Doctor Mike.

"WOOF!"

What else does Doctor Mike do?

Examines sick animals in the vet's office.

Operates on animals.

Gives vaccinations.

Tests samples in the lab.

What does Doctor Mike need?

Warm clothes

Vet's bag

Stethoscope

Scissors

Lab coat

Bandages

Medicines

Disposable gloves

Syringe

Rubber boots

other busy people

Here are some of the other busy people vets work with.

Farmers breed and look after lots of animals—sometimes thousands! Each and every animal needs to be kept happy and healthy.

Animal rescue workers care for pets who have been lost or neglected. They also look after wild animals who are sick or injured.

Zookeepers feed and care for many different types of animal from all over the world. They make sure that the animals are healthy and call a vet if there are any problems.

Veterinary nurses work in a vet's office caring for sick animals.